COLOR THIS BOOK

SAN FRANCISCO

BY ABBI JACOBSON

CHRONICLE BOOKS

SAN FRANCISCO

Haight-Ashbury

The Painted Ladies, Alamo Square

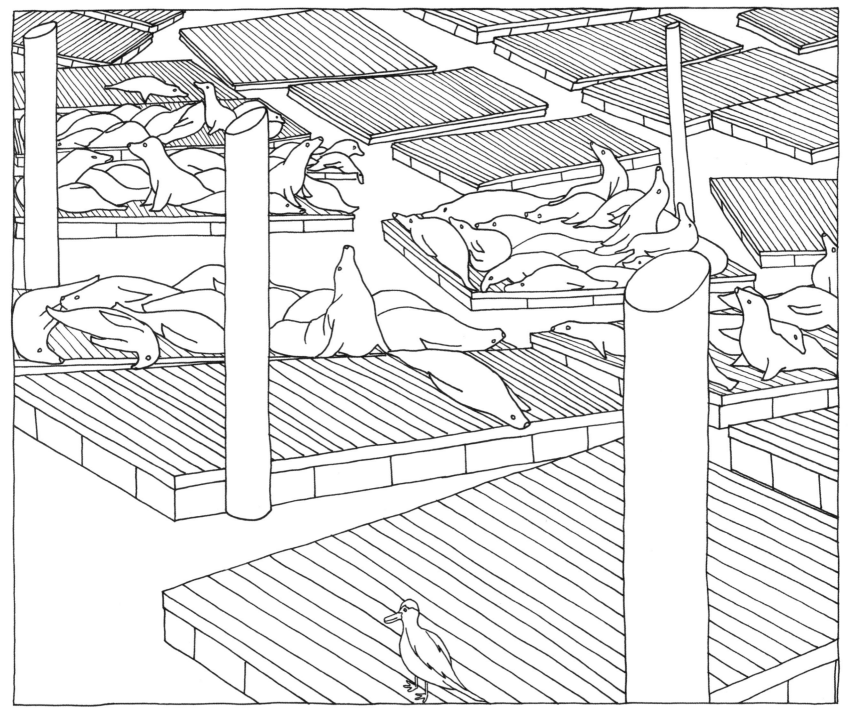

Pier 39 and the Sea Lions, Fisherman's Wharf

Amoeba Music, Haight-Ashbury

City Lights Books, North Beach

Mission Dolores Park

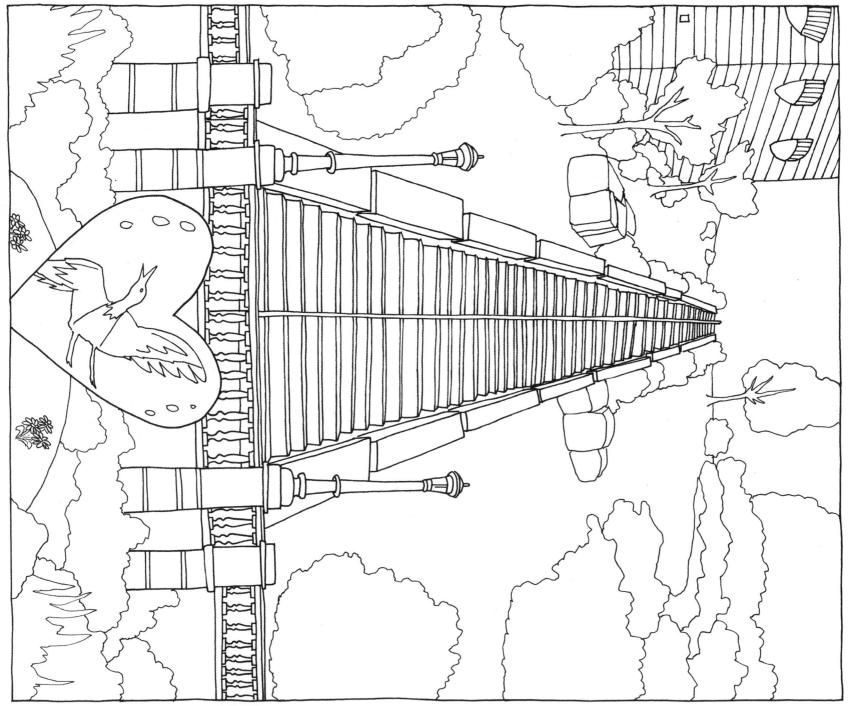

Lyon Street Steps, Pacific Heights/Cow Hollow

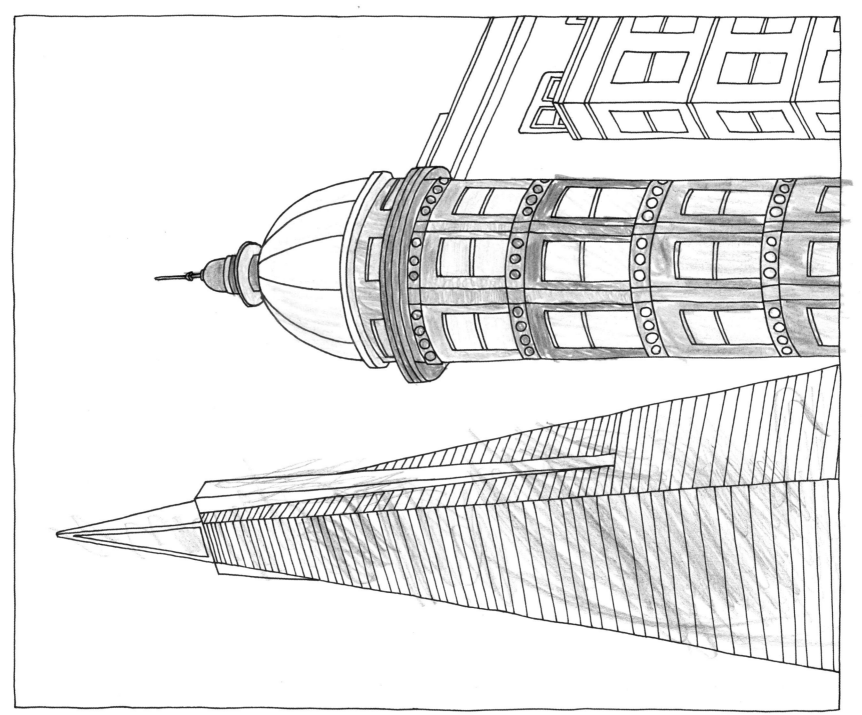

Transamerica Pyramid and Columbus Tower, Financial District/North Beach

Souvenir Magnets in Chinatown

Ghirardelli Square, Fisherman's Wharf

Ferry Plaza Farmers Market, Embarcadero

A Crab Stand, Fisherman's Wharf

Union Square

La Taqueria, the Mission

Coit Tower, Telegraph Hill

Hyde Street Cable Car and Alcatraz Island

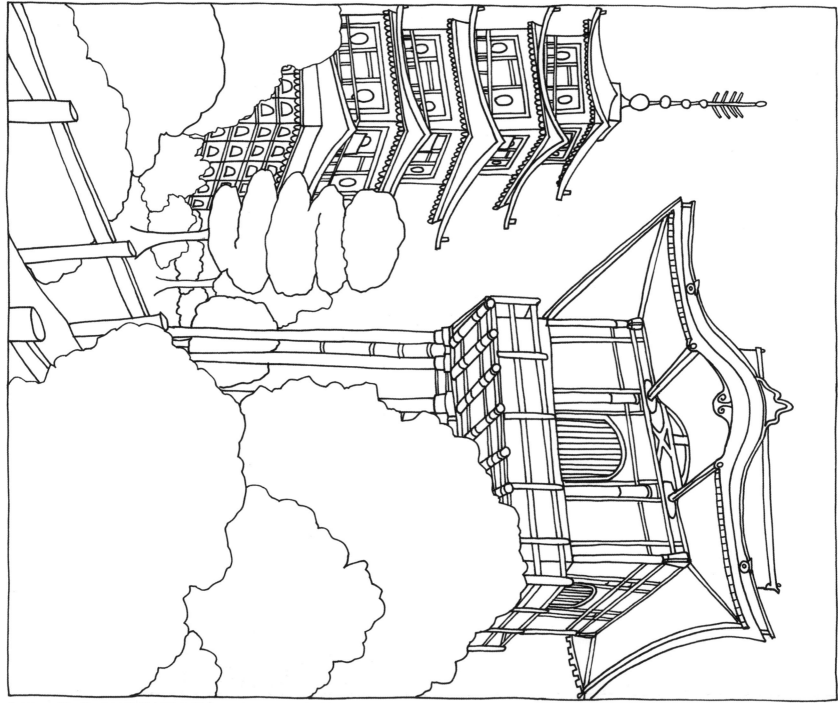

Japanese Tea Garden, Golden Gate Park

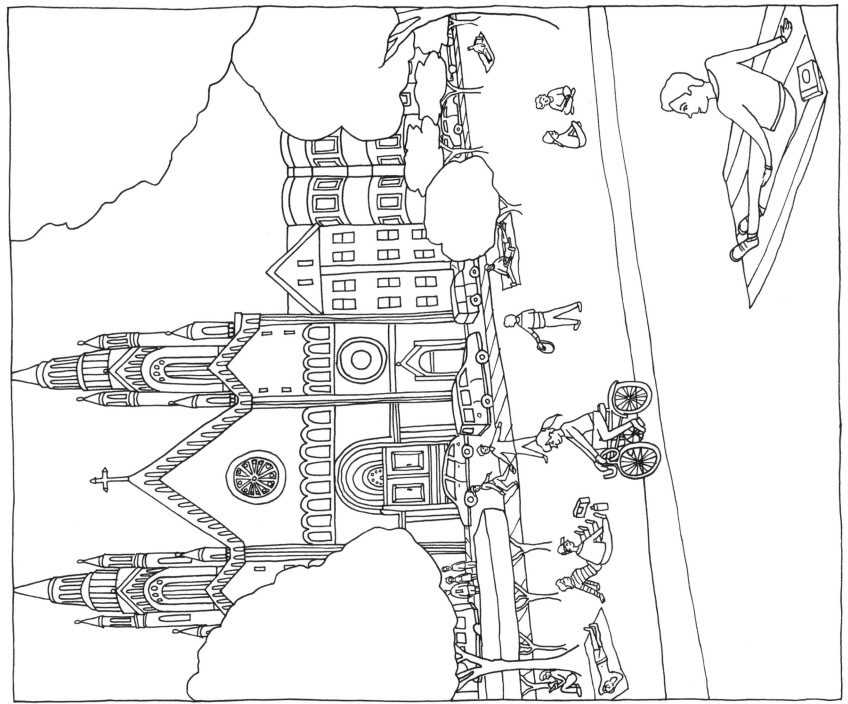

Saints Peter and Paul Church/Washington Square Park, North Beach

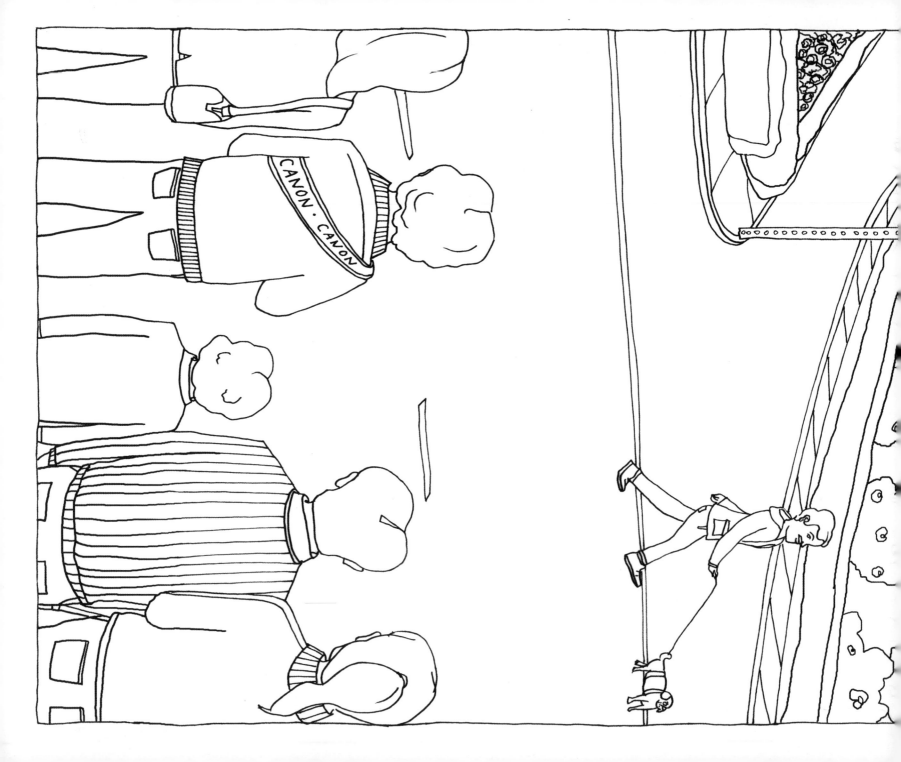

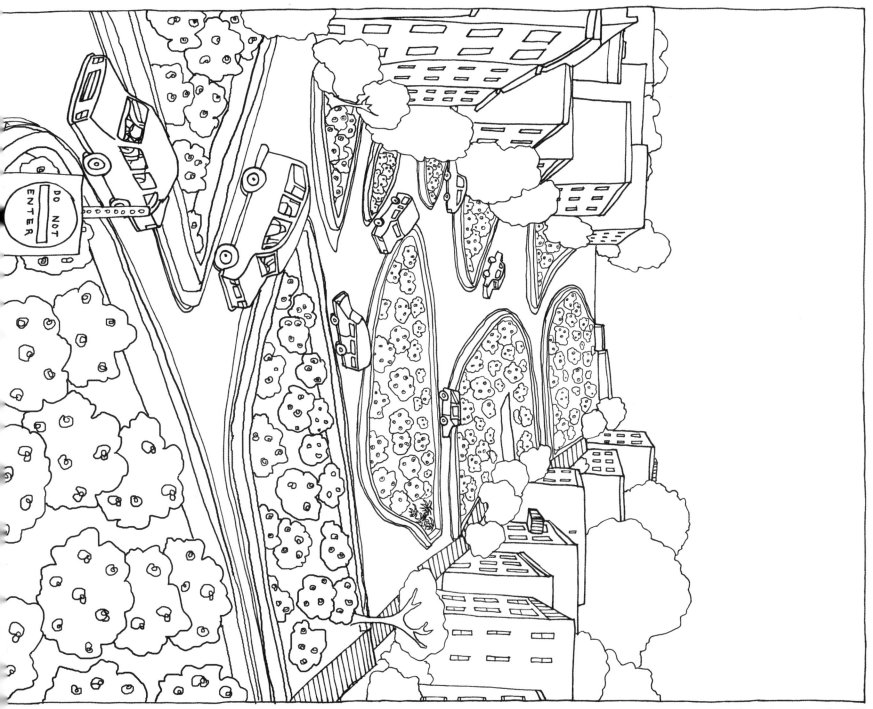

Lombard Street, Russian Hill

Burma Superstar, Inner Richmond

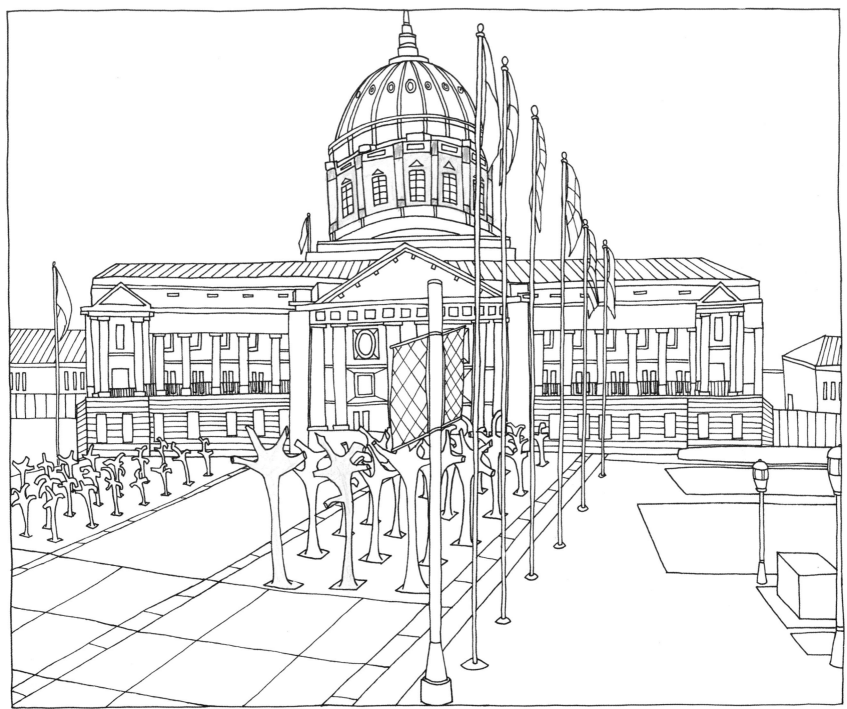

City Hall, Civic Center

The Castro Theatre, the Castro

Bi-Rite Creamery, the Mission

Dottie's True Blue Cafe, Tenderloin

Golden Gate Bridge

A San Francisco Hill

Dragon Gate, Chinatown